MEDITATION

God Speaks and I Listen

Sri Chinmoy

Copyright © Sri Chinmoy Centre
Second edition, 2019

Artwork: Sringkhala Lucina Della Rocca Hay
Author photo: Piyasi Morris

All rights reserved. No portion of this book may be reproduced without express written permission from the Publisher.

ISBN 978-0-9957531-5-0

Blue Beyond Books Limited
4 Paget Road, Ipswich
IP1 3RP, United Kingdom

www.bluebeyondbooks.co.uk

Printed in Great Britain

MEDITATION

God Speaks and I Listen

by

Sri Chinmoy

Editorial note

This book presents Sri Chinmoy's answers to questions on meditation from spiritual seekers, university students and luminaries from all walks of life. They are complete and unabridged.

Editor's preface

Many people are discovering in meditation a way to find peace of mind and a more centred focus on their true inner nature. In these volumes, spiritual teacher Sri Chinmoy answers a wide range of questions about the world of meditation, including the meaning of different meditation experiences, how to make meditation practical and the intrinsic value of meditation.

Sri Chinmoy normally taught meditation in silence, through the inner contact he established with a seeker. However, over the decades that he spent in the West, inspiring and instructing both his own students and the public, he was approached on innumerable occasions for specific inner and outer guidance. His answers have illumined aspirants from all backgrounds. This collection of questions and answers represents a portion of that dialogue.

God Speaks and I Listen

What is the best way to meditate?

Sri Chinmoy: The best way to meditate is to feel that you have come from the Source. This Source is Delight. When you meditate, feel that you have come from that Source and you go back there triumphant and victorious. Here on earth you play your role and then you go back to the Source. The Indian scriptures say:

Anandadd hy eva khalv imani bhutani jayante
Anandena jatani jivanti
Anandam prayantyabhisam visanti

> From Delight we came into existence,
> In Delight we grow.
> At the end of our journey's close,
> Into Delight we shall retire.

This is the ultimate way of meditation.

How do I begin meditation?

Sri Chinmoy: First of all, you have to study a few spiritual books to get inspiration. These should be written by real spiritual Masters and not by fake spiritual teachers or by aspirants who are still on the path and have not yet attained illumination. Spiritual books and scriptures will tell you how to physically and mentally discipline your life to some extent. You can take the help of these books for a few days or a few months.

Then you will realise that your book-knowledge of meditation is not enough. You will want to have the solid experience of genuine meditation. Now, each person has to have a meditation of his own. If you want to go to the end of the road and reach your inner Goal, then you should have the true meditation of your soul. This meditation will help you reach the destined Goal. You will need a spiritual teacher, a Master who can give you a meditation according to your soul's qualities. The Master can tell the seeker inwardly about his meditation by asking the soul to come to the fore and telling him through his soul how to meditate, or the Master can tell him personally when he sees him. If a spiritual Master gives a meditation, then that meditation is undoubtedly the best that the aspirant can ever have.

If you don't have a Master, you should go deep within and get your meditation from the inmost recesses of your heart. The meditation that gives you immediate joy or continuous joy is the best meditation for you. Everyone will not have the same meditation. Your meditation will not suit me, my meditation will not suit you. You like a certain food, I don't like it. You are right in your own way, I am right in my own way. But once you know what your best meditation is, please stick to it. In your mind or in your aspiring being, try to formulate a few meditations. Today you can try one way of meditation, then you can try another way of meditation tomorrow. If you have seven types of meditation, you can try one each day. At the end of one week the one that has given you most satisfaction or abiding joy is your best meditation.

Even if you do not want to study spiritual books and do not care for a spiritual Master, then first and foremost you should keep the mind calm and quiet, and let the soul speak to the mind about what it actually wants. If the mind is calm, we can receive the light of the soul in the mind. The light enters into the mind also through the heart. When we meditate collectively we do this kind of meditation.

I always recommend that one should practise concentration; otherwise, meditation will never be fruitful. When we sit for meditation, millions of thoughts and ideas will enter into our mind and disturb us. We should practise concentration for a couple of minutes and then enter into meditation. For some seekers who have been practising concentration and meditation for a long time, concentration is no longer necessary; they can immediately enter into meditation. To have a calm and quiet mind is not easy. It is most difficult. It can be done only by the Grace of God and through the most sincere aspiration. If one has inner cry and if God's Grace descends, then only can proper meditation be practised and achieved.

When we are learning to meditate, what sort of questions should we ask?

Sri Chinmoy: There are several questions a seeker should ask himself when he is learning to meditate. "How should I meditate?" "Why do I want to meditate?" "What kind of meditation do I want?" "What do I expect to do when I meditate?" "How sincerely have I accepted the spiritual life?" "How much time am I prepared to spend?" When we have the highest form of meditation, however, we do not have to ask any questions. The best form of meditation is to transcend the mind. Right now from the mind we are getting good and bad thoughts, but a day will come when we have to enter into the highest Truth. At that time we shall not allow any thought or question to enter into us.

If you feel that you are a beginner, you should control your mind. You should try to be alert, with your eyes open, and focus all your attention on the heart. If your aim is just to have a little peace of mind or a little harmony in your family, the conscious will of your heart is all that is needed for the time being.

If you have meditated for a number of years and feel that you are not a beginner at all, then only your dynamic will to reach your Goal will help you. If you say, "I want to have the highest meditation so that I can realise God the Absolute," meditate on your heart. But you will have to spend quite a few hours daily in the highest meditation if your goal is to realise the Highest. When you meditate, how can you stop the functioning of your mind? Try to consciously lose your individuality and personality. If you can consciously lose them, the soul of your meditation will take care of the illumination of your life's aspiration. Only illumination will breathe in you and around you.

I would like to know what teaching you give for obtaining a good state of meditation?

Sri Chinmoy: There is no hard and fast rule. There is not one kind of meditation that everybody has to do. You have to meditate according to your development and according to the needs of your soul. Each patient has his own medicine; each individual has his own way of meditation.

Whenever a disciple of mine comes to me and says he has not yet discovered his way of meditating, if I see that he is sincere, I tell him to come and see me. I meditate with him first for a few minutes, and then I tell him how to meditate. The meditation is meant only for that person. It is given in strict confidence. If that person tells others I won't be the loser; it is he who will be the loser. Each person must go his own way during his meditation because each one has a particular role, a special mission on earth to fulfil. In God's divine Lila, His cosmic Play, everybody cannot play the part of a king or queen. But each one has been allotted a particular part. And to perform that part one has to meditate according to his own inner necessity.

Some seekers feel that what they actually need is love and devotion for God. They feel that to enter into the mental world, to approach God through the mind, is a waste of time. These seekers pray with the heart. But there may be others who like to pray with the mind. Basically, if somebody wants to be very intimate with God, like a child with his mother, then he has to approach through the heart. If one wants the knowledge and wisdom of God, if one wants to know what is happening on which plane and so forth, he has to approach with the mind.

When one has reached God, when one has God, the path ends. At that time we do not say, "I came through this path and he came through that path." Once we are in God's Consciousness we get the benefit of all the paths. That is to say, if I follow the path of devotion and you follow the path of the mind, when we have reached the ultimate Goal, we get the same thing. But according to our propensity we should follow a particular path. There are various ways. You have to go your way and I have to go my way. But ultimately we reach the same goal.

In order to practise meditation with one Master, do you advise giving up all the other spiritual paths?

Sri Chinmoy: When practising spiritual disciplines under the guidance of a spiritual Master, it is always advisable for you to follow his path exclusively. You have to give up other paths once you accept his path. If you are satisfied with this Master and are still looking for another Master, you are making a mistake and are acting like a fool.

How should I do meditation if I have never done it before?

Sri Chinmoy: First try to be calm and quiet at least three times during the day: in the morning, at noon and in the evening. You don't have to actually do any kind of meditation. Just feel that these five minutes belong to you and nobody else. Act like a miser. Feel that you are not going to give these five minutes to anybody, not to your relatives, your friends, your enemies — nobody.

These five minutes are absolutely yours. When you are with yourself, this is not self-centred ego. Here "you" means you in your highest form. Your highest form is God, and you are growing into this highest form.

If you have friends who know how to meditate and you meditate with them, even unconsciously, your inner being may receive inspiration from them. If you are a very sincere seeker, then you will get help consciously in the form of inspiration from your friends who are sitting beside you. You will learn things from your spiritual friends. Automatically the power of meditation in you will increase.

You have to know that in your case the power of meditation is not strong enough right now for you to continue meditating for a considerable time, fifteen minutes or a half an hour. But the main thing is not to become discouraged. When you begin taking exercise, you cannot do it for more than five minutes. But if you practise daily, then after a few months you can take exercise for an hour or two. What we need is regular practice at a regular time. If you can meditate early in the morning at a particular hour, then try to continue meditating every day at that hour. At that hour God will knock at your heart's door. Open it and He will offer you His Peace, Light, Bliss and Power.

Regularity is necessary. Although we are regular, we may not give first importance to our meditation. But if we give importance to our meditation and are sincere, whole-hearted and dedicated in our spiritual life, automatically our power of meditation will increase.

I have never been to your Centre before. I have read a few books but I'm a beginner in meditation.

Sri Chinmoy: You are coming here for the first time, and you have read many books but have not meditated before. Books have given you the inspiration to enter into the field of aspiration. Here we are all aspiring to reach the Highest and fulfil the Highest.

In the spiritual life, when you are in the presence of a spiritual Master you receive according to your capacity of receptivity. You are a beginner, but that does not mean you will be denied something. Everybody was a beginner once upon a time. A beginner in any school cannot sit together with someone who is far advanced because their lessons will clash. But in the spiritual life

MEDITATION

we have to feel our inner oneness with those who are ahead of us. We also have to feel how far and how deep we want to go.

Those who are my disciples do not need special meditations because I have taken the responsibility for their meditation. How? I have simplified the matter. There is a photograph of me in my highest transcendental Consciousness. A seeker should always meditate on what inspires him most. Just because I am their Master, my disciples get abundant inspiration from meditating on this picture. If anybody looks at it with love, joy and devotion, no matter how much of a beginner he is, no matter which path he followed before, just because the person is a seeker, my inner consciousness will open its door to him. On our path if anyone devotedly concentrates a few minutes each day and enters into my third eye, then I take responsibility for his meditation. During his meditation at home, if the seeker is attuned to me, I will immediately feel that a voice is coming from within and telling me that that person meditated at this hour and so forth.

You are a beginner, but you don't have to be doomed to disappointment. Your sincere cry can make you swim in the sea of aspiration. The easiest way to meditate for my disciples is to concentrate on my picture. You can try it just for a couple of days. If you have faith in me, which is of paramount importance, I can assure you that your life of real aspiration can immediately begin. It is your own sincerity that will easily expedite your inner search for ultimate realisation. You are a beginner at this moment. At the next moment you need not be a beginner. A beginner is a drop. If the drop consciously throws its existence into the ocean, then the beginner immediately becomes an expert, advanced and accomplished seeker.

Is it good for one to be with other spiritual people?

Sri Chinmoy: If you have a Master, then his inner guidance is bound to strengthen your aspiration. But if you do not have a spiritual Master, then you have to read books written by spiritual Masters and mix with seekers, with spiritual people. There are many others who are seeking and practising meditation but do not have Masters. In the spiritual life also, "Birds of a feather flock together."

If you see that a thief or some other culprit is sitting beside you, then automatically your consciousness will descend because of the vibrations coming from him. Negative, undivine forces will come and attack you. But if you mix with those people who are leading a spiritual life and are trying to realise God, they will undoubtedly strengthen your aspiration. If you have faith and trust in these people, their very presence will inspire you. If you sit beside a spiritual person, he will be thinking of God, meditating on God, on divine Love and divine Peace. And this Peace and Love will enter into you also. So the best thing is always to mix with spiritual people as much as you can.

I attend the meditation here at the college once a week but I feel I need more spiritual nourishment. If I try to meditate alone, it's different. I feel that there is something I am losing.

Sri Chinmoy: You are not actually losing anything. When four persons do the same thing together they inspire one another. It is like a tug-of-war. When you are meditating with your group, there are four or five persons meditating together against only one person: ignorance, whereas when you meditate at home, you are one individual and ignorance is another individual. You don't know who is going to win in the tug-of-war. When four persons are pulling on one side and only one is against them, you know that these four are going to win. This inner assurance will encourage you to come and pull with the others. If you meditate at home alone, you are fighting against ignorance all by yourself. Naturally you will soon be exhausted, and then you will feel sad and miserable, and may lose interest. But if you can meditate with others, then you will have more confidence in what you are doing.

A little ripple
Wakes the sea.
A tiny thought
Shakes the world.

Why do we have to meditate every day?

Sri Chinmoy: It is very simple. Every day you eat; that is why you live on earth. You cannot live on the food you ate yesterday. Similarly, the divine child in us also needs nourishment every day. Every day you have to feed the soul. Meditation means the conscious feeding of our soul. If we eat every day, we become very strong because of our regular nourishment. So also when we meditate every day the soul is being nourished. Then it gets the opportunity to manifest itself better, that is to say, to manifest the Divine on earth. This is why daily meditation is necessary.

I have recently become your disciple. Does what you say about meditating when you get up apply to disciples or do you have a different standard for them?

Sri Chinmoy: I expect all my disciples to meditate in the morning before six-thirty. From two o'clock to six-thirty I concentrate on all my disciples. At that time my soul, my existence, my consciousness are responsible for feeding you. After six-thirty my inner beings take the responsibility. I am not saying that my inner beings are inferior to me; no, they are not. But if you want to give me joy in the physical mind, then please meditate before six-thirty. If you meditate after six-thirty my inner beings will have to take care of you. And again, if you meditate in the evening or at night, my inner beings and your inner being will commune.

Why should someone meditating alone in his room be bothered by the agitation of the world outside in the street, especially if he can't hear it from his room?

Sri Chinmoy: Once the day dawns, Mother Earth becomes divinely energetic or undivinely restless. Especially in the West, because of its present dynamic nature, there is some feeling of irritation in the cosmos, or in the outer nature. These restless qualities of the world do not have to enter into you, but usually they do. When people move around, immediately their vibration enters into you, no matter where you are. The air, the light, has already been corrupted by human toil, human anxieties. The world is standing in front of you like a roaring lion. How can you enter into your highest meditation in front of a roaring lion? But, if you can meditate before nature starts functioning, when the cosmos is still and the entire universe is taking rest, then you will be able to get a more powerful concentration and a deeper meditation.

Why is it necessary to have flowers, incense and so forth in order to meditate?

Sri Chinmoy: When we offer flowers, when we burn incense, light candles and take a shower before meditation, we convince our physical that we are doing something. The outer life and inner life must always go together. But the outer is not the ultimate. The ultimate is inner aspiration, the mounting flame within us. We have to be aware of our aspiration, and then constantly go within and fly to the highest level of our consciousness. Flowers, incense and washing before meditation also help us to have purity. The purity of the body is of paramount importance in the spiritual life. It is in purity that God's breath abides. If physical purity is lacking, then it is simply impossible for the Divine to breathe in you. Purity demands cleanliness in the body. What we call cleanliness in the outer world we call purity in the inner world. So before you start meditation, no matter when you meditate, take a shower or wash your eyes, ears and nose and feet with cold water, and if possible use flowers and incense to create an atmosphere of purity.

Should a person be alone when he meditates, or does it have anything to do with environment? Do you advise him to be in a big crowd or do you want him to shut himself away all alone?

Sri Chinmoy: He who meditates has to act like a divine hero. He has to serve and while serving he is guiding. He is serving the divinity in humanity. One has to face the world and not retire into the Himalayan caves. We have to act like divine heroes here amidst humanity. Humanity is part and parcel of God. By throwing aside humanity, how are we going to reach divinity, which is part and parcel of humanity?

MEDITATION

What we need is transformation. We have to accept the world as it is now. If we don't accept a thing how can we transform it? If a potter does not touch the lump of clay, how is he going to shape it into a pot? The world around us is not perfect, but we are also not perfect. Perfect Perfection has not yet dawned, but we expect to attain perfection through our meditation. How are we going to discard our brothers and sisters who are our veritable limbs? I cannot discard my arm. Similarly, when we meditate soulfully, devotedly, we have to accept humanity as our very own. We have to know that humanity as it stands is far, far, from perfection, but we are also members of humanity. We have to take it with us. If we are in a position to inspire others, if we are one step ahead, naturally we have the opportunity to serve the divinity in the ones who are following us. We have to transform the face of the world on the strength of our dedication to the divinity in humanity. Meditation is not an escape. Meditation is the acceptance of life in its totality, with a view to transforming it for the highest manifestation of the divine Truth here on earth.

Can we meditate while lying down? Is this not the best way to relax?

Sri Chinmoy: For meditation you do have to relax. And for a spiritual person who has meditated for many years and knows how to meditate at his command, lying down and meditating for hours is no problem. But for the beginner, or for the person who is not advanced in meditation, lying down will present a problem. This type of meditation is not dynamic or active. His blood circulation will not function properly and a very subtle kind of drowsiness will attack him. But when he is in a sitting position, drowsiness cannot assail him. The very act of lying down takes us into the world of coma. Then what happens is that we feel we are meditating most sincerely and dynamically but we are wrong. I had a cousin who is now twenty-five or twenty-six years old. She used to tell us that every night she would meditate at least ten hours while lying down. My sisters used to enter into her room and find her snoring. They would then pull her hair, nose and so many things. But she would not wake up. The following morning she would say that she meditated the whole night. She did not have conscious meditation. It was an unconscious way of feeling that she was meditating. Meditation is very good; but this kind of meditation while lying down tends to lead toward self-deception about one's own spirituality. It is better to meditate while sitting or even standing. While walking up and down, to and fro, you can also meditate. I used to meditate in a very relaxed way two or three hours or more while walking very fast, like the marching of a soldier.

I don't seem to feel comfortable and relaxed while meditating in a sitting position.

Sri Chinmoy: Everybody has a room where he can meditate. He may not own a house or apartment, but he certainly has a room. In one corner of that room he can have a shrine where he can sit and meditate. When the body feels uncomfortable it will change its position and it is up to you to keep it comfortable. If there is restlessness though, immediately relaxation goes away. If you constantly move from this side to that side, how can you have relaxation? In order to maintain relaxation, one has to keep calmness in the body and avoid restlessness at all costs.

Is the lotus position the most comfortable one for meditation?

Sri Chinmoy: According to some the lotus position is the most comfortable and again according to some it is not. The main advantage of the lotus position is that it helps the spinal cord to remain erect. Otherwise, the lotus position will not necessarily keep your body relaxed. We can stay for two or three hours in the lotus position, but if one wants to meditate for four, six or eight hours, I don't think he will be able to sit for that long in the lotus position, but he can make his body relaxed in many other ways such as walking in a relaxed manner or sitting in a relaxed manner.

*My meditation-heart
Is the sole producer
Of my life's excellence.*

I read a book about concentration and meditation that said one should pay attention to the direction one faces while meditating, whether East, West, North or South. If one wants spiritual things and a quiet life, one should always face North. If one wants worldly things one should face East.

Sri Chinmoy: It depends on the individual. A sincere spiritual seeker who wants to realise God and God alone does not need any particular direction. He has to be infinitely above all such Indian traditional theories. For God-realisation what we actually need is aspiration in the purest sense of the term.

I wonder if you could tell me something about inner discipline.

Sri Chinmoy: Discipline should come from inside. Outer discipline is necessary, but if there is no inner discipline, then outer discipline has no value. Outwardly I may be calm and quiet, but inwardly I can be cherishing all kinds of wrong thoughts.

If you want spiritual discipline, then you have to know how to concentrate. Concentration is of paramount importance in disciplining us. Every day you eat. Every day you go to school and every day without fail you should practise concentration. What will you concentrate on? You will concentrate on the life that is fulfilling and not the life that is disturbing or destructive. What can build your life? Your cry for God. If you want to possess the world, then you will not be able to discipline yourself. If you want only to be possessed by the Inner Pilot, by the Supreme, then only you will be able to discipline yourself.

To start meditation, do you discipline yourself through will or do you joyfully start?

Sri Chinmoy: The soul is a divine portion of God and is all joy and cheerfulness. Now, if you start your meditation through discipline and keep your body very tight and straight, as if a monkey who is full of evil thoughts is trying to bite or pinch you, it is wrong. By doing this you become afraid and you only keep yourself tense. What you should do when you meditate is to allow yourself to be relaxed, keeping the spinal cord erect. The best way is to meditate in the lotus position, but if you cannot do this, then just sit on a chair.

God is all Love and Joy. The most effective way to please God and to become one with God is to approach Him through love. And where there is love, there is joy. To go to my Father, I do not have to cut off my hands or arms to show how self-disciplined I am. That is no discipline at all. Discipline comes through spontaneous love. When we allow our divine qualities to come to the fore, automatically the soul takes care of our outer life. We just have to go deep within and from there we shall have to bring out the soul's poise. When the soul's poise comes to the fore, automatically the restless outer being becomes calm and quiet. So please try to meditate always with inner joy.

How do you go about emptying your mind in order to be able to meditate?

Sri Chinmoy: First, you have to aspire. Then, you have to make your mind vacant. You should not allow any thought to enter into your mind and take shape. Suppose a name comes. As soon as the first letter of the name appears, you kill the name. You have to make your mind vacant, as empty as possible.

How do you do it?

Sri Chinmoy: With your power of concentration. Suppose a thought, or a vibration, or something else is coming. Immediately, shoot an arrow and pierce it into pieces. An idea comes, somebody's name comes, or some thought comes. Immediately, just throw it out. It must not come and enter into your mind. Before it touches your mind, you have to cut it into pieces. But if you already have thoughts and ideas within you, within your body, within your mind, then you have to meditate like this: be as relaxed as possible. Feel as if you were inside the ocean. Then absorb those thoughts and ideas so they do not have a separate existence. They are lost in the sea. If they are already within you, throw them into the sea. If they are coming from outside, then do not allow them to enter into you. After doing this your meditation is bound to be successful.

Q

Can we do our meditation without doing concentration exercises first?

Sri Chinmoy: If you want to learn meditation without going through concentration, you must feel that you are standing at the door of your inner room. When you stand at the door you allow only your friends to enter into your room. You do not allow strangers or your enemies.

You have to welcome only good thoughts, divine thoughts. These are your true friends. Undivine thoughts, hostile thoughts, must not come into your mind. Your mind is constantly receiving thoughts and you have to be very careful. You have to welcome only divine thoughts. Then play with these divine thoughts. Let them play in the garden of your mind. Play with thoughts of divine qualities, divine Love, divine Power or divine Peace. Let them play, let them grow. While playing you will grow into the divine aspects of Truth. Then a time will come when you will see that there are no thoughts, if you allow only divine thoughts to play within you. Your entire being will be surcharged with inner Divinity. Your consciousness at that time will try only to be receptive. And what will descend, what will enter into you? Truth in abundant measure, Light in abundant measure, Love in abundant measure, everything in infinite measure.

I am a musician and I would like to know your ideas on concentration. When we study music, we realise that we need a great deal of concentration. I would like to know how you develop concentration.

Sri Chinmoy: I would like to know what you mean by concentration.

To me, concentration is awareness. The more I can concentrate on something, the more aware I am of it, the more I can grasp all the details. If I am not concentrating enough on something, I cannot understand it completely. I feel concentration also means leaving oneself a little to the side, but I would like to know your opinion.

Sri Chinmoy: Concentration is not the same as awareness. If you want to achieve extraordinary concentration, please try this. Take an idea and try to make this idea into a living being. Then place it on the wall at your eye level. If it is too difficult to use an idea, then take some material object and place it on the wall. Keep your eyes open. It is always better to concentrate with open eyes. Look at the object and start concentrating. Now enter into the object. You have to apply all your attention and pierce through the object to the other side. When you have gone to the other side, from there start concentrating. You are there, your body is here. You start concentrating from the other side and from there look at your own body.

First you try to focus your attention on a particular object, then you enter into it, then you go beyond it. At this time, you become the witness, or sakshipurusha. This is real concentration. This is the secret of meditation. If you know it you can concentrate most effectively.

To be one's witness is the secret?

Sri Chinmoy: One's own witness.

It is very difficult in that way?

Sri Chinmoy: It is difficult.

It is as if you were there, standing there looking at yourself?

Sri Chinmoy: Yes, but first you have to enter into the object and then go beyond it. Then you come back to yourself and become the witness.

I'd like to develop better concentration so that I can keep my mind focused on one thought.

Sri Chinmoy: Before you start your meditation I wish you to repeat the name of God, "Supreme," about twenty times as fast as possible. First purify your breath by repeating "Supreme." The breath has to be purified; unless and until the breath is purified, the mind will wander and cannot remain one-pointed. If the breath is purified, then the mind will not act like a restless monkey.

Then I wish you to concentrate on your inner divinity. Always try to feel that you are safe when you are with God, with divinity. Let God and the divine qualities within you act against your human, undivine qualities. When you use the word "God," please try to feel your real love for God. When you are concentrating, feel that you are really growing into God, into the very breath of God. Then your concentration is bound to do something for you.

Next I would like you to focus your attention on a picture. You can look at my picture or you can look at yourself in the mirror. If you concentrate on your own reflection, try to enter into the image that you are seeing. You have to feel that you are totally one with the physical being that you see. From there you should try to grow. How will you grow? You will grow with one thought: God wants you and you need God. Repeat: "God wants me, I need God. God wants me, I need God." Please try to do this. Then you will see that slowly, steadily and gradually God the divine thought is entering into you and permeating your inner and outer existence, giving you purity in your mind, in your vital and in your body.

How do you apply that way of concentrating to a chapter of a book that you have to study?

Sri Chinmoy: Do not take it line by line. When you concentrate on a chapter it will be several pages, but you can only see two pages at a time. But this is what you do. Suppose there are ten pages that you have to commit to memory. Just hold these pages; do not read them. Just enter into them and then go beyond them. Before you start reading anything in an ordinary way, word by word or line by line, just concentrate and take it

MEDITATION

as a whole object, not scattered lines or a series of lines. Then concentration is very successful. Then it becomes very easy to learn anything by heart. Here the witness is the person who does the concentration. When I was a student, at the age of fourteen or fifteen, in my history class I used to commit thirty or forty pages at a time to memory by the power of concentration. The teacher used to ask me, "How do you do it?" Of course, I could do it in various ways. There are a few Sanskrit mantras for this. If you just repeat these mantras four or five times, then just read any poem twice, a fourteen or sixteen or twenty-line poem, and you can easily prove that you have learned it by heart.

I would like you to teach me that mantra.

Sri Chinmoy: When I was a student I had to study French. One of my sisters was very fond of me and at the same time she used to cut jokes with me. We had to learn a French poem, about twelve lines. I was the youngest, so naturally I was bragging, boasting, "Look, I can do it!" My sister also knew French well. She said,

"No, you can never do it." So I said, "Look, I will read twice any poem that you give me. Then I will show you that I know it." She brought the book, and picked out a very difficult poem of sixteen lines. She said, "Now you have to prove that you read it just twice. You have to read it out loud, otherwise how can I know how many times you are reading it inwardly?" I said, "First give me a minute. When I start reading I will read it out twice, but before that you have to give me time to concentrate." So in front of her I concentrated. Then I said, "Now give me the poem." She brought it and I read it just twice and then I recited it. She was very pleased, and then she said, "Now teach me."

I said, "I am not the person to teach you."

The difficulty is that unless and until you are commanded by the inner being, or by God, you cannot tell these things. My sister is my dearest, but I cannot tell her because I am forbidden. In other things I can give my whole life for my sister, but this I am not permitted to tell. Once I gave this mantra to one of my friends, a most ordinary friend. He was a student, but he found it very difficult to memorise. He was very dull, so I taught him, gave him this knowledge. God asked me, otherwise I could not have done it.

How can we meditate better each time?

Sri Chinmoy: You know that each time you take exercise your muscles become stronger and stronger. If you can do one push-up one day, the next day you will try to make it two push-ups, and then you go on and on increasing daily. You come to thirty or forty push-ups. Then a time will come when you can do fifty. Let us say fifty is your maximum, that is your highest. Then what will happen? The Grace of the Supreme will allow you to make it fifty-one. You see the world records in the Olympics. They are all broken. The Olympic record of four years ago is shattered like a piece of glass. So you should practise every day to transcend your previous achievement.

If you want to make your meditation better, you have to feel a need, a divine need. You have to know how close you want to become to God. You have to have the inner cry to be inside His Consciousness all the time, to be totally merged in Him. If you have that kind of feeling, then try to feel that today you are a hundred steps away from your Goal, and that tomorrow you will be only ninety-nine steps away.

Is meditation our duty?

Sri Chinmoy: Yes. We should try to feel our daily duty to the Supreme's mission in our morning meditation. All our activities should be directed toward our supreme duty. When you are at work in the outer world, during the day, you have to feel that it is your duty to aspire. You have to know how many minutes you are in a divine consciousness. It is your duty to work and support yourself and pay attention to your household responsibilities. But this is not enough. This is your human duty. If while you are working your mind, your consciousness, is on God, then you are thinking of the divine duty. When divine thought and divine action go together, divine thought will act like a pioneer; it is immediately followed by action. Immediately duty is performed. You have to feel your outer actions are inspired by divine thought, divine knowledge, divine Light. Then it will be divine duty.

Otherwise it is only a waste of time from the spiritual point of view.

What do you mean when you say that dedication is meditation?

Sri Chinmoy: Dedication to whom? When you feel you are giving something to someone, helping people, this is not dedication. Dedication means feeling God's conscious presence in the other person. If you are working and at that time you are feeling God's conscious presence, this dedication is a form of meditation. But if you feel that you have some capacity to inspire or help someone even though you do not see God's presence inside that person, then you are only aggrandising your ego by letting it tell you that you have more inner wealth than the other person. If you are doing something and at the same time feeling God's Presence in the work itself, then that dedication is meditation. But if just because of your own ego, you feel that you are a little better or superior and you are going to the other person to help him, then that is no dedication, that is no real meditation at all.

What happens if after meditating for a while, you decide you want to take a rest and then continue your journey at a later time?

Sri Chinmoy: In the ordinary life, after you have covered one mile you can remain where you are for a while and take rest before continuing on your journey. But, in the spiritual life it is not like that. In the spiritual life, once you take rest, doubt enters into you, fear enters into you, suspicion enters into you. All kinds of negative forces enter into you and destroy all your possibilities. Your potentiality remains the same; eventually, you will realise God. But the possibilities that you once had, the golden possibilities, you have lost. If you stop meditating and leave the spiritual life, the progress that you have made will be destroyed. People will not receive a good vibration from you; nobody will get inspiration from you; you won't be able to give your soul's smile. You will fall back to your old ways and be lost to ignorance. However, the essence of the progress that you made remains inside the soul. The essence is never lost, even though in your outer life you cannot use it. The quintessence of the progress that you made will remain inside your heart, and after five or ten years, when you want to meditate again, or in your next incarnation, this quintessence will come to the fore. If you pray to God most sincerely to enter into the spiritual life again, your previous progress will loom large in your life.

So always be on the alert and run as fast as you can towards your Goal. Do not stop until the race is won; otherwise, the pull of ignorance will take you back again to the place from which you started.

Do you pray sometimes?

Sri Chinmoy: To be quite frank with you, I do not pray. And also, I have no need for meditation, but I do meditate for my disciples. After one has realised the highest Truth, one has no need to pray or meditate. But I have a few hundred disciples, and I meditate for them as I used to meditate for myself more than twenty years ago. When I meditate on them, prayer is automatically there, because I am trying to help them in their spiritual awakening, in their spiritual aspiration and realisation. In deep meditation, prayer is present.

Is there a method whereby if one does not have patience for meditation, he could use hypnosis or self-hypnosis instead to quiet the mind so his soul can come forward?

Sri Chinmoy: To try and approach meditation by way of hypnosis is dangerous and negative. The better way is to dive deep into yourself. Through hypnosis one doesn't go into himself. When all other aspects of the person, the heart, the vital, the physical, join in really going deeply into one's soul, then there is a chance of quieting the mind. The human mind though can never convince the soul. There is no reason for the soul to be enticed by the mind. The soul does not push. The soul has infinite patience. But sometimes, if it is God's Will, the body, vital and heart can force the mind to diminish its activity.

*As your heart
Is meant for deeper things,
Even so, your mind
Is meant for higher things.*

Do you feel pain while you are meditating? Do you feel any pain? If someone hit you, would you feel pain?

Sri Chinmoy: If it is the highest type of meditation, we will not feel any pain because at that time we are not in the body, but in the soul. If our consciousness is in the physical, if somebody pinches us immediately we will feel pain. But if we are in the soul, we will not be affected. The soul is the divine part in us, the divine Light, which is the representative of God. This soul cannot be disturbed, cannot be destroyed. It is something in us that is immortal. When we are doing our highest meditation, we are not in the physical; we are in the soul. We become one with the soul.

Here we are living in ignorance. That is why somebody can come and strike us. But if a person is in the Light, he will not bother us. He will not disturb us. He will never pinch us. On the contrary, when he sees that we are meditating, he will come and also start meditating with us because he feels that we are doing something good, something divine. Naturally, he also wants to do the same things so that he can be a divine child.

Could you recommend some books on meditation, concentration, contemplation and aspiration?

Sri Chinmoy: Are you interested in following the path of any particular spiritual Master? Because spirituality is a very vast and varied subject. You have to know whether you want to go on the path of devotion or through pure, abstract ideas. You have to know what path you are going to follow. Then you will be in a position to derive the utmost from a book. Otherwise if you study it may be a waste of time.

If you are interested in Sri Ramakrishna, the great spiritual Master of India, or if you want to study the path of the Vedanta and the Upanishads, then you can study the spiritual writings of Vivekananda, Sri Ramakrishna's dearest disciple, and some of his other disciples' books. If you want to follow the path of integral Yoga, integral acceptance, then study the works of Sri Aurobindo. If you would like to study from the spiritual point of view, then you can read the books of India's ex-President, Dr. Radhakrishnan. His books will certainly clarify Indian thought and help you to fathom Indian teachings.

If you are interested in concentration, contemplation and meditation and you want to know the specific method used hundreds of years ago and the secrets of meditation, you can read the Samkhya Shastra of Kapila and the Yoga Sutras of Patanjali. There you will get mental information as well as meditation.

If I meditate on a person, can I be with him on the inner plane?

Sri Chinmoy: Certainly you can. If you have an intimate friend who is absolutely sympathetic to you and your inner life, you can try this with him: you have to enter into him and you have to breathe simultaneously with him. If two sincere, dedicated, aspiring souls sit together every day and practice breathing together, they will achieve the result. You should count one, two, three, and breathe in at the same time. Then stop counting. When you are breathing in, feel that he is also breathing in. Look at one another and converse through the eyes. If you can develop identification this way with two persons sitting face to face, then you can throw this same power of identification all over the entire world. Even if the person is separated from you, thousands of miles away, you can easily know what he is thinking.

This inner identification is practised by all spiritual Masters. Every day in the morning and in the evening and at other times also, I use this power of identification for my devoted disciples in different parts of the world. Then I see, hear, know everything they do. There are many minor things they do which I do not take into consideration, but when there is something very serious, before it actually touches the physical, I try to destroy it on the mental plane. As far as your question is concerned, this can be done, and I must say, it has to be done by all sincere aspirants and especially by leaders who want to serve and help humanity, no matter in which field; the spiritual field, the political field or any other field.

Is it possible to go directly to the formless Supreme, or do we have to invoke the Supreme with words such as Aum?

Sri Chinmoy: We have to go from the form to the formless. A seeker cannot go from the formless to the form. When we go to church and pray, we utter the name of God or of Christ. We know that Christ came into existence, he descended to earth and took a human form like us so his Truth could be seen. Similarly, when we chant Aum we invoke the Trinity: Brahma, Vishnu and Shiva, that is, the Creator, the Preserver and the Transformer, and these all have form.

But can we use Aum to enter into the formless?

Sri Chinmoy: You not only can, but also must do this. You know that in music you can sense the finite and also the Infinite. The finite, which is the form of the music, is what you use to enter into your music. Once you have entered through the finite, you will feel that the music is taking you to the Infinite. But you are starting with the finite. So also in your spiritual life, if you start with the name of God, it helps a lot. After a few years or so you need no longer utter God's name, you enter into the consciousness itself. When we are in our deepest meditation, we do not utter the name of the Supreme or God or anybody. At that time, we simply exist in our oneness with Him.

In our deepest meditation, God sees our aspiration and at that time we do not have to ask for Peace or Light. We need not utter the name of God, because He knows what we are crying for. As a mother knows what a child is crying for, so also when we are in our deepest meditation, God, who is our Mother and our Father, knows what we need.

How should we meditate on the picture of a spiritual Master?

Sri Chinmoy: When we meditate in front of the picture of a spiritual Master, we should try always to identify ourselves with the consciousness of the spiritual Master which is embodied in the particular picture. If we want to identify ourselves with his consciousness, then the first thing we have to do is to concentrate on the whole picture. Gradually, we should bring our focus of attention to only the face, then to between the eyebrows and a little above, which is where his actual inner, spiritual wealth can be found. This is the third eye, the place of vision, and the moment we can identify ourselves with the vision of inner reality, we shall achieve the greatest success.

If you want to get purity as you look at the picture, imagine that you are breathing in simultaneously with the Master for five minutes before you start your meditation. You should feel that he is also breathing — the Master and disciple must breathe in together for five minutes.

Can you tell us how a beginner can meditate on an aphorism like the one you just read out?

Sri Chinmoy: Yes. Today's meditation was:

> I need an illumined mind
> To study God's entire Life.
> I need a devoted heart
> To feel God's immortal Love.
> I need a surrendered soul
> To realise God's infinite Joy.

Now, which are the key words? First, "illumined mind." The sophisticated mind, the intellectual mind, the doubting mind, the frustrated mind we see every day. But I used the term "illumined mind." What is the illumined mind? It is the mind that is surcharged with Light. The moment the mind is surcharged with divine Light, it is illumined. If there is no Light or very little Light in it, then it is merely the sophisticated, intellectual, doubting, frustrated and destructive mind.

The next key phrase is, "to study God's entire Life." Our human life is the short span of sixty, seventy or eighty years. But God's entire Life means Eternity, which has neither beginning nor end. To think of something beginningless and endless we need an illumined mind, for the ordinary mind cannot begin to comprehend these ideas. The ordinary mind cannot think of even two things at a time, not to speak of concentrating on two things at a time. But with the illumined mind, we can think of twenty things at a time.

These phrases have given you an idea of what you should think about — God's entire Life — and what you should strive for — an illumined mind. Allow these thoughts and aspirations to come into you and create a world of their own. Then you will see that you are meditating on something sublime. From reading something soulful and inspiring — this aphorism — you have received a clue about what is worthwhile to think about and also about how you should think about it.

"I need a devoted heart to feel God's immortal Love." Human love we know does not last. It is the experience of a fleeting second. But immortal Love, God's immortal Love, lasts forever and will always fulfil both you and humanity. Everybody's heart is good and pure. Our mind and vital may be bad, and they may obscure the heart. But the heart is always good. Very often we mistake the vital for the heart and say that someone has a bad heart. But this is not true. Everybody has a wonderful heart, but that heart functions properly only when it has devoted qualities, like a mother's heart. A human heart may be pure and sincere, but only when one has a devoted heart will one try to serve God, realise God and fulfil God. There are many people who do not utilise the heart to dedicate and devote themselves to the spiritual life. For these people, real progress is impossible. The heart that is not devoted will be constantly moving from one object to another. Only the heart that is dedicated and devoted can feel God's immortal Love.

"I need a surrendered soul to realise God's infinite Joy." Everybody has a soul, but unfortunately the face of surrender we have not yet seen. For a fleeting moment someone may surrender to somebody else: a wife may surrender to her husband, or a husband may surrender to his wife. But a surrendered soul is one that is totally surrendered, constantly surrendered, for an entire lifetime, if not for Eternity. God has and is all divine qualities, but His most important quality is Joy or Delight. If one wants to see God's infinite Joy, then one has to make complete surrender, total surrender, unconditional surrender. One has to grow into a surrendered soul. Unconditional surrender is not the surrender of a slave to the master. Unconditional surrender is conscious, willing and cheerful surrender. The aspirant surrenders to God's Will because he feels that by surrendering to God's Will, he is becoming one with God Himself. Conscious and unconditional surrender is what God wants from each person on earth. If the seeker can surrender himself entirely to God's Will, then he will feel God's infinite Joy in him.

I have explained this aphorism in my own way, but you can have your own way of interpreting it. After you have read some soulful spiritual writings, or the meditation for the day from one of my books of spiritual aphorisms, please try to meditate on them or allow divine thoughts and ideas to enter into your mind. Pick the key words or

MEDITATION

ideas, like, "illumination," "God's Life," "devoted heart," "immortal Love," "surrendered soul," "infinite Joy," and so on. Then open your heart and let the thoughts come. If you really focus on these divine ideas, undivine or silly thoughts cannot bother you, because your mind will be in the world of illumination. If you are sincerely thinking of illumination, only illumination can enter into you. If you think of a devoted heart, only devotion will enter into your mind and your consciousness. If you think of a surrendered soul, it is a surrendered consciousness which will enter into you.

Meditation can be done in this way for the beginner. If you are a beginner, at least you have started, so do not worry about your present capacities. No matter where you are, start. This is the first way of entering into meditation. Gradually the time will come when you will have no thoughts, no ideas, no mind during your meditation. Neither divine thoughts nor undivine thoughts will enter into you then. Only Reality, eternal Reality, will grow within you.

How can one have inner peace in the outside world?

Sri Chinmoy: For that one has to meditate regularly. Before you enter into the outer world, you are at home, in your own room. You stay at home and you sleep for five, six or seven hours At that time you are the boss. There is nobody to interfere. There is nobody entering into your mind. If you want to, you lock the door, you bolt it from inside and do not allow anybody to come in. This is in your outer, earthly existence: you have a room and you do not allow anybody to enter into it. Similarly, you can close your inner doors, the doors, let us say, of your senses when you have fully strengthened your inner being. Your inner being can be strengthened as you strengthen your muscles. If every day you take exercise, you will see that your muscles become strong, stronger, strongest. In the spiritual life also, before you enter into the turmoil, the hustle and bustle of life, at home you should meditate regularly for fifteen minutes or half an hour.

Now, each time you meditate, please try to feel that you have gained some strength, inner strength. And this strength is something solid. It is not your mental fabrication. You meditate for ten minutes and then go out. If you see two people who are fighting, your inner peace may not enter into them, because they are now in another world; but your inner peace has enough strength to protect you. You will not be affected. That doesn't mean that you are very cruel or indifferent to them, you are worse than these people who are fighting. It is not that you are not sympathising while they are being hurt. No. They are fighting, they are torturing each other, but you will see it as a scene in a drama or a play. Your inner being, which is the real reality inside you, will not be affected. On the one hand, you will see that they are doing something wrong. On the other hand, you will see that you are not doing the thing yourself. If we do not follow the spiritual life, what will happen is that immediately we will take one side. "This fellow is sincere, this fellow is not the culprit, the other fellow is the real culprit." Or, we will have a kind of undivine quality within us. We will notice that this undivine, aggressive quality is coming forward. We feel that if we also had strength, we would strike somebody. When we see undivine people, if we are not spiritual, or even if we are spiritual, sometimes our undivine qualities come forward. But if we are really spiritual, our own spiritual qualities come forward and these divine qualities, like a thief, want to enter into those who are using undivine qualities, quarrelling and fighting.

When we come out of the house into the world, we have to be well protected. Not with armour. No, we will be protected with divine thoughts, divine ideas, a divine Goal. The moment we have a goal, we shall walk only towards the goal. We have a destined goal and we are running towards the goal. There are many people who are watching us, and sometimes they are mocking at us. They say that our speed is not satisfactory, or in various ways they mock at us. This world is like that. If we are not one of them, immediately they will think that we are indifferent or we are insane. But if we know that we have a goal of our own, and we are running towards the destined goal, no matter what they say or what kind of life they are leading, we will not be affected. The divine in us will protect us and at the same time if the divine in us wants to offer a little Light to those who are wallowing in the pleasures of ignorance, they will get some light from us.

But early in the morning we have to meditate. Everybody has to meditate. This early morning meditation is of paramount importance for a spiritual seeker. If we go out without morning meditation, we are bound to feel, if we are conscious, that we are facing a roaring lion. But if we go with a very sound, solid meditation, after we have had a very good meditation, we will feel that a dog is following us, our most faithful dog. Our inner being will be surcharged with indomitable Peace, Light and Power. If we don't go with meditation, the roaring lion is going to devour us. If we go after having a most successful meditation, inwardly we will see that the world of aspiration or even the world of suffering, depression, and despair sees something in us. It tries to follow us, sometimes with reluctance, sometimes with joy, sometimes with greed, but in some way or other it tries to follow us like a dog.

Does one achieve divine experience through meditation?

Sri Chinmoy: Through meditation we are bound to get divine experience. Meditation is the means. If one meditates, certainly one will get divine experience. If one doesn't, then one will have only ordinary, human experiences. Meditation is the only answer. Meditation is the key to enter into the divine world.

You said your talk was based on your inner experiences. How did you get these experiences?

Sri Chinmoy: From meditation. From my concentration, meditation and contemplation. I was in a spiritual community for twenty years. Similarly, if you spend fourteen, sixteen, twenty years in spiritual practices, naturally you will also get inner knowledge in abundant measure. From the ages of twelve through thirty-two, I went through rigorous spiritual discipline: concentration, meditation, Yoga. It took me eight hours, ten hours, twelve hours, fourteen hours of meditation daily to achieve what I have right now. When you study in school and get your master's degree, you start offering your knowledge to the world at large. In the inner life, also, when one concentrates, meditates and contemplates, one enters into the world of inner Wisdom, inner Light. From there he can bring to the fore at his sweet will the Light, Bliss and Power that he has achieved and offer it to others.

This morning during my meditation
I had a glimpse of my soul
For the first time.
Never before have I seen
Anything so beautiful.

Should outer experiences be considered transitory?

Sri Chinmoy: Each experience helps us but at the same time we do not remember each experience in detail. We do not keep the whole experience in the outer world; we keep the essence of the experience in the inner world. The experiences you had at the age of twelve are unknown to you now. In your outer life you have totally forgotten them, but in your inner life their essence remains. In the inner world nothing is lost; everything is recorded. In the outer world, an experience is real for a while, and then a few days later it is totally defaced. Before realisation, certainly all is transmuted in the outer life. It does not stay in our day-to-day consciousness. But in the inner life the real essence remains.

Are the little sporadic experiences that we have during meditation part of realisation, or are they small steps to realisation?

Sri Chinmoy: In a sense each experience is taking you to realisation; each experience is a step towards realisation. But again, if instead of walking slowly, one has the capacity to run very fast, then one need not have thousands or millions of experiences before realising God. Each experience certainly helps us; it gives us confidence, it gives us joy. Somebody may say that he wants to eat a mango today, an orange tomorrow and another fruit the day after. Before he gets the fruit that he calls the goal, he will get many little tastes of fruit. But only when he eats the fruit that is his goal does he get full satisfaction. But again, if somebody is absolutely sincere in saying that he does not want anything but realisation, he will say, "I don't want any other fruit. I want only the fruit that is meant for me, the fruit that is my goal, the fruit that will offer me complete satisfaction."

How can I have a transcendental experience in my meditation?

Sri Chinmoy: If you want to have transcendental experiences, you need a special meditation, as well as inner discipline. Just by doing something intensively you will not necessarily get what you are seeking. Suppose you dig at a place where there is no water. You may dig and dig, but if there is no water, what will you do? But, if you dig at a proper spot where there is water, you will get it. Similarly, if you have the proper meditation, proper guidance and proper self-discipline then certainly you will have the transcendental experience.

Sometimes while meditating I have the feeling that I am looking everywhere. What does this mean?

Sri Chinmoy: While you are meditating you are looking everywhere. Your consciousness at that time is expanded. You are not only one person among many on earth; you feel that the whole world belongs to you and that you belong to the world. The world can claim you at that time as its very own. Right at this moment you cannot claim the world as your own at all. Your brother, your sister, the rest of your family — these are yours, but that is all. But when you feel that you are seeing everything around you during your meditation, everything is yours, everyone is yours. Inwardly you can claim everything, and everything that is around you can claim you also as its very own. This is a very good experience.

When I meditate, I often feel that my ego gets in my way.

Sri Chinmoy: We have a human ego and a divine ego. The divine ego is called our inseparable oneness with the universal consciousness. In the divine ego our "i" becomes universal; we become larger than the individual self and establish a feeling of oneness with everyone. When you meditate, if the ego comes forward, then feel that you are the universal "I" instead of the little "i".

Once during meditation I had the experience that I was neither inside nor outside. There was no solidity; there was nothing concrete, objective or real. I didn't know where I was or what was happening.

Sri Chinmoy: This is a good experience. You were neither inside nor outside. Then where were you? When you are not inside, that means you are not inside your highest reality. And when you are not outside, that means you are not in your outgoing energy. The inside has the message of purity and the outside has the message of beauty. You have not entered into the very depths within, where purity looms large, and at the same time you have not entered into the very depths without, where beauty is manifested. When inside becomes purity, then outside becomes beauty. Now this is one way of experiencing the truth. But another way of experiencing this truth is to feel that you are standing somewhere holding the outer world of imperfection and the inner world of perfection. You are the bridge in your life between the outer world and the inner world where you are neither the outer world nor the inner world. You are bringing the inner world into the outer world so that it can manifest itself, and you are taking the outer world into the inner world so that it can realise itself.

A friend of mine who is a pianist had an experience that he told me about. He was playing a passage on the piano, a very fast arpeggio, and suddenly he realised that without reducing the velocity of the passage he could stop and look at every note he was playing. He looked at the notes as though he was looking at what he was doing from another plane where time had not the same dimension as time has here. He was playing very fast and all the time he was looking at what he was doing. There seemed to be no relation to the time concept that we have in this plane. Would you say that this was a case of concentration?

Sri Chinmoy: It was not concentration at that time. His soul was playing and having communication with two worlds. He was not concentrating on anything. His soul was communicating with two worlds and he was just observing it.

While meditating I sometimes feel that my body is moving rhythmically, but when I open my eyes I see that I am not moving at all.

Sri Chinmoy: This is a very good experience. The movement that you feel is in the inner world, in your subtle body. When you open your eyes, you become aware of your physical consciousness. The reality has not yet manifested itself in the physical nor does it need to manifest itself. If you feel that you are flying while you are meditating, you don't have to manifest this movement in the physical. A bird and an aeroplane can both fly, but their consciousness is not higher than yours.

If you feel abundant Peace within you, then immediately try to manifest it in your eyes, in your physical consciousness. If you feel Light, try to manifest it. Very few people have Peace here on earth. If you have Peace, immediately you are solving the problems of the entire world when you bring Peace into the outer world, when you manifest Peace. The world needs Peace, the world needs Love, the world needs Joy, the world needs all divine qualities.

In the subtle body I can fly, but I do not need to fly on the physical plane; a bird and an aeroplane can perform that task. My joy is to see and feel Peace, Light and Bliss and bring them to the fore in my outer life. By manifesting these divine qualities, I can be of great help to mankind and fulfil God.

When I start to go deep within, I feel sleepy.

Sri Chinmoy: It is not sleep; you are making a mistake there. While you are meditating, your mind is entering into the world of calmness and silence. There you don't have to create any movement or be dynamic. This world of silence is not like ordinary sleep, where one becomes totally unconscious. On the contrary, it is a very good state. Try only to grow into that state with utmost sincerity, humility and devotion.

However, if meditation proper has not yet taken place, if you feel sleepy when you are merely preparing to meditate, it means that inertia and sloth are present. But if it is after a good meditation that this feeling comes, it is not sleep at all. You are entering into the world of silence and mistaking it for sleep.

Sometimes in deep meditation I feel my whole body going completely numb as though it has been anaesthetised. I can move only my eyes.

Sri Chinmoy: This is a very good experience, the experience of silence. The mind has totally surrendered to the heart during your meditation. The heart takes the mind with it, and both surrender to the soul. At that time what you get is a feeling of static silence. Try to stay in that silence; do not be afraid of it. You can stay there for a couple of days or even a month without any fear. And that silence will grow into dynamic silence. You will feel that in the silence itself there is spontaneous creativity, spontaneous movement, spontaneous life — the life of spiritual awakening, spiritual experience and spiritual revelation.

Sometimes during concentration at twilight, for instance, I hear a vibration which is like a murmur or a hum. Is that vibration from my own subtle body or is it the vibration of the earth, of the atmosphere?

Sri Chinmoy: The vibration comes from your subtle body. It does not come from outside, particularly in your case.

Is the feeling of the soul coming out of the body something to have as an aim? What will happen to the body if the soul does not come back into it?

Sri Chinmoy: When we say that we want to bring our consciousness out of the body during meditation, we do not want to kill or destroy the body. We have to bring the limited consciousness out of the body and throw it into the universal Consciousness.

Our aim should be to come out of the finite and enter into the infinite. During our meditation we feel all-pervading peace, joy, bliss and power which we do not normally feel. The moment we think of the body, we are limited; we are in a prison cell; we are only five feet and a few inches tall; but the moment we think of the soul, we will feel Infinity, Eternity and Immortality all around.

There are two approaches to the high, higher, highest levels of consciousness. If one wants to work in the world or for the world, no matter how high he goes, the Divine will grant him the opportunity and the assurance of coming back into the world. Because the Divine wants this seeker to work for Him and manifest Him here on earth. But if one does not want to manifest here on earth, he will be given the chance to stay in the higher worlds. His soul will not have to come back into the body.

There is no need to think about bringing one's soul back into the body. If you work for the world, then God Himself will pave a clear, sunlit path for your return through your meditation. Your meditation takes your soul or consciousness out of your body, and also brings it back. No matter where you go, since you have accepted the world and want to work for the world, the meditation that takes you to the highest will bring you from the highest to reveal and fulfil the Divine here on earth.

Sometimes when I look at the sunshine and I close my eyes, I see a round disc in front of my eyes with the blossom-colour that is described by some writers as the colour of the vital body. Is that my own vital body?

Sri Chinmoy: At times you see the reflection of your own vital body and at times you see the reflection of the object you are looking at. Each object has a subtle part. Even a wall has a subtle part. Although you are seeing the form of the wall, behind the wall or within the wall, there is a subtle form. You see the subtle form coming forward.

Guru, can the quality and colour of light that one sees in meditation be used as a guide to the height and quality of the meditation?

Sri Chinmoy: Yes, it can be, but only if you know the significance of the light or colour can it be of help to you. If you know the significance of a colour you have seen in your meditation, then you will be able to know whether you are making progress in your spiritual life or not. Suppose you are meditating very deeply and you see blue light; you know this light is from your meditation, and not from your imagination. When you know it is from your deep meditation, immediately feel that this blue light is the light of spirituality. This light means you are becoming as vast as the sky, the vast blue sky. Again, the light means you are consciously becoming one with Infinity. If you do not know the meaning of the blue light, you will simply notice what a beautiful wonderful colour it is. It will help you to a limited extent, because your inner being does make progress when you see blue light. But if your outer being knows what the colour signifies, then your progress, your evolution, proceeds much faster.

The same holds true when you repeat mantras, and when you chant Sanskrit slokas or verses. If you know the meaning of the slokas and chant them soulfully, you get the utmost benefit from them. There are many scholars who know the meaning of the slokas, but they do not chant them soulfully. Like a parrot they repeat the mantras; they do not get any result from their chanting. A seeker may not have studied the slokas thoroughly like the scholars, but if he knows their basic meaning and he most sincerely, most devotedly prays and meditates on them, he gets the utmost benefit. There are many people who have studied the Indian scriptures. They know that blue signifies vastness; red, power; gold, manifestation; white, purity; green, freshness and dynamism. They know these facts, but they do not meditate on the colours, and they get no result. Now there are sincere seekers who meditate on the colours without knowing their significance. They will definitely derive benefit from their meditation, but if the conscious mind knows the significance, they can get the utmost benefit. Suppose you have seen a blue light. For ten days or even for two months that experience can keep your consciousness very high and vast. If your inner being has a special connection with the Indian spiritual Master, Sri Krishna, then you will say, "Lord Krishna's colour is blue." By identifying with him, immediately you will get something from him, consciously or unconsciously.

To my disciples I would like to say that I represent all the colours and all the lights, but my most prominent colours are blue and gold. Whenever you see any colour, please feel it is an indication of inner progress. There are some seekers who see light when physical eyesight is failing. When my brother was losing his vision, he used to have wonderful visions in red, blue, and white. He did not meditate like the rest of our family. The doctor asked him to please go to an eye specialist. This does not apply to you, far from it — only to those who do not consciously pray and meditate.

Sometimes you may see a light that need not be connected with you at all. During sleep or meditation, your inner being may contact someone else's inner being, and the light you see is not your own, but his.

Suppose that during meditation you have become totally one with your daughter. You are not meditating on her, you are meditating on the Supreme, but one of your inner beings has suddenly made a very close connection with your daughter, although your physical mind is not aware of it at all. If at this time you see green light, because green signifies dynamism and new creation you may think that a new creation has dawned in your own life. You will expect yourself to be very dynamic and fresh. Then, when the next day you see that old ideas are still bothering you, you will curse yourself. You will say, "After I had this experience, how is it that I am still dwelling on old thoughts? I cannot come out of the prison-cell of my old life!" Unfortunately, you do not know that this experience is not telling you something about your own inner life, but about your daughter.

Quite often it happens that when we are very close to another person we identify ourselves with him. We feel that something which is actually going to happen in that person's life will be taking place in our own life. But if we are very conscious during our meditation, then we will be able to make the distinction. The person who is dear to us does gain something when we see his light, and consciously or unconsciously he gets joy. But if we tell him about the experience so that his conscious mind knows that we have seen his light, then he will derive the most benefit from it.

If you feel that by keeping your eyes closed you can see the blue light sooner, then you have the right to keep your eyes closed. But you have to know whether you will make the fastest progress by seeing the light or by keeping your eyes open and identifying yourself with my divine consciousness. You may feel, when you see the blue light, that that is all, that you have achieved everything. But I wish to say that seeing any light of any colour need not be the ultimate achievement, or the best experience. For my disciples, it is most important to establish oneness with my Light. If you feel that blue light is more profitable than identifying consciously and soulfully with my consciousness, it will be a mistake. But if you feel that since the blue light comes spontaneously to you, you can make tremendous progress, then certainly you are doing the right thing. It is up to each individual to feel how he can make the fastest progress.

What is the significance of seeing a very blue light during meditation?

Sri Chinmoy: A blue light is the light of Infinity. To see blue light around yourself or someone else means that your inner being is responding to the vast Infinity, that your spirituality is mature and has entered into your inner and outer existence. This is a very good experience, a very high experience. White light is spirituality; blue light is also the light of pure spirituality, the light of the Infinite. To see blue light around some spiritual Masters, for example, Lord Krishna, means that blue is their predominant colour, although some spiritual Masters have all colours in their aura.

On different occasions I have seen red, white, blue and yellow lights. Could you please explain the significance of these?

Sri Chinmoy: Red is the dynamic aspect of God, the divine power which you are seeing inside yourself. When the red colour of Divinity's Power enters into you, you are energised; power flows through you.

Now white is the colour of purity. When you see white all around you and above you, you will feel your whole physical existence inundated with purity. You are not impure, but when you see white, in your whole existence, from the soles of your feet to the crown of your head, you become pure. When you see a pale blue colour, try to feel that Infinity is entering into your aspiring consciousness. We cannot think of Infinity as just a term in our mind. Our mind will imagine a great distance, expand it a little farther, and then stop. But when we aspire with our soul, we can really expand our consciousness into Infinity itself. Infinity goes on expanding like a bird spreading its wings endlessly. When you see blue, try to feel that your consciousness is expanding into Infinity, and Infinity is entering into your aspiring consciousness. This pale blue colour is the favourite colour of India's greatest spiritual Master, Lord Krishna.

Now what you may call yellow, if you use your inner vision, is really golden. This golden colour comes from the highest realm of Consciousness. At times, when you see this golden colour in the field of manifestation, it is absolutely red, whereas if you go to the source, it is all gold. Manifestation takes place here, in the earth-consciousness, not above. This golden colour is the colour of manifestation when it starts in the highest plane. Then when it touches earth, it becomes red. Visions of colour come for two reasons: real aspiration and Grace from the deities and from the highest Absolute.

In India we have a goddess called Kali, Mahakali. I am most fond of this Mother-aspect of God. When she enters into the vital world of human beings, which is full of emotion and turmoil, her golden colour becomes red, because she is destroying all imperfections, limitations and wrong forces in our lives. What you see in the psychic world as purely gold, in the vital world you will see as red.

Each aspirant has what you call in the West a guardian angel. God is always there, but each of us also has one or more presiding deities. In your case, when you see light you have to feel that some angels are showing you the light to protect you, guide you and lead you.

I cannot say anything about the angels since I do not even know their names, but in your Indian incarnations, Kali was your presiding deity. Those who have had Indian incarnations are bound to have an Indian presiding deity. According to Indians, there are gods and demigods, apart from the one absolute God. "As many souls, so many gods." Your presiding deity, from the Indian spiritual point of view, is Kali, since the Power-aspect of the Supreme is predominant in your nature. This does not mean that you will not love humanity or God's creation. You will offer love and joy, but you will express love for humanity through dynamic power. Love is absolutely pure, but here it is being expressed through power. One can also express power through love.

Meditate silently.
You will be able to create
A totally new life
For yourself.

Would you please speak about the aura seen in meditation?

Sri Chinmoy: Meditation has nothing to do with auras. Each individual human being has an aura which you may see during your meditation, but you may also see your aura during concentration or even during sleep. There is no direct connection between meditation and the aura, but while you are meditating you are in perfect peace and it becomes easier for you to see your aura. A spiritual person can enable you to see your aura, or you can do it in your own meditation, but there is no direct link between meditation and the aura.

The first time one of my disciples came to me she thought she saw my aura while I was standing in front of her. I have to be frank: It was her own aura that she saw in her spiritual Master. She became part of my consciousness and her aura was reflected in my body.

If one does see the aura there is no harm; it inspires the seeker and gives him great joy. But to waste one's time in search of an aura is nothing short of stupidity.

About four years ago, when I came in contact with this philosophy, I dreamt that I saw a tent descending from Heaven. In the tent there was a man from India. I saw his face, and he had a lighted candle in his hands. Does this dream mean that I have to meet that person or that he had something to do with me in another life?

Sri Chinmoy: This spiritual man had previous links with you. In India, we know and believe that each human being has a special connection with some spiritual figures besides God. We call them presiding deities. You have more than one presiding deity observing your day-to-day activities. You do not see them, but they are observing you and guiding you. The spiritual figure you saw is one of those who are helping you in life. He was kind enough, or you were in a very high state of consciousness, so he appeared to you as a human being from the inner plane.

You mentioned that one of your disciples had seen your face of a previous incarnation during meditation. Why would he see a previous physical body?

Sri Chinmoy: One can get an inner experience, an inner vision from looking at a picture. People can get different experiences depending on what is within them. When one identifies with my consciousness, this is not only the consciousness of this incarnation, it is the consciousness of millennia which is constantly growing. When consciousness is embodied in the physical, it is easier to grasp it and be convinced that it exists. I have this physical body, previously I had other bodies, but deep inside me there is a soul. Ordinary people cannot see my soul, but they can see my physical form. When this disciple looked at me, it was impossible for her to see my all-pervading inner consciousness; she got the vision of a past incarnation of mine to convince her physical consciousness that I take different names and different forms. When we are in this physical world, we understand everything that exists in the terms of form. All-pervading consciousness cannot be given any decisive form, but if it is necessary for the sake of comprehension, God allows a human being to see a past incarnation.

When you see someone's soul in a dream or vision, you very often see his present body as you know it, but if you go deep into a soul with whom you had some past connection, you may see his former body. That is what happened in this case.

When I am looking straight into your eyes and you are looking into my eyes, I see your face go out of focus and you disappear completely. Afterwards your face appears, and then it disappears again. What does this mean?

Sri Chinmoy: When you look at me you think you are seeing my physical body, but you are seeing my universal Consciousness. You make contact with life itself in its different forms. Then when you come back to your own consciousness, my face comes back into focus. When I am looking into your eyes, speaking to your soul; you are seeing me through the eyes of your soul.

When I meditate, I imagine you giving me a blessing at that moment. Is this blessing real?

Sri Chinmoy: Yes. When you meditate and you feel that I am blessing you, this blessing is absolutely real. But it is not my physical being that is blessing you, it is my inner being, which is totally one with me. It is like a storehouse in which I know where everything is kept. I bless my disciples with the help of my inner beings. When you see that I am blessing you, this experience is absolutely real. My physical mind may not know that this is taking place, but my inner being will definitely know. The most important thing is for my inner being to know what is happening in your life. My physical being sees only what is around me, but the subtle beings inside my physical are now in New York, in Canada, and in many other places. They are roaming and bringing me news which is all being recorded. But if there is something very important, absolutely urgent, these subtle beings will bring the news to me even while I am talking. They will ask me to stop talking and they will let me know what has happened.

Was the Peace and inner Bliss that I felt here last Wednesday night a sign that I had been initiated?

Sri Chinmoy: Last Wednesday I did not intend to actually initiate anybody, but when you stood in front of me, your soul immediately recognised my status and, like a child of two years, your soul threw itself into my lap and received all the blessings — Bliss, Peace, Love and Power — from the Supreme. I emptied the inner cup that was full of ignorance and impurity and replaced them with Peace, Bliss and Purity. Although this was not a formal initiation, I can say that you were initiated that night.

MEDITATION

The night I met you I had a very dramatic experience. During the meditation you came over to me and put a flower into my hands. My hands weren't moving at all, but there seemed to be a tremendous power that was pulling them. I was looking at you and I thought, "What is he pulling me for?" Then when you looked at me I felt as though my inner being was whirling around and exploding through the top of my head. Can you tell me what this means?

Sri Chinmoy: Your outer world burst into pieces and entered into the inner world, where you have not only accepted me, but felt and realised my spiritual achievement and realisation. Your outer world of turmoil finally surrendered to your inner world of spiritual infinitude. This is a most beautiful and high experience.

When I went home after I first saw you, I entered into a kind of dream where you were the only person who existed, and my whole body was decomposed into raindrops. Could you explain this?

Sri Chinmoy: Your entire existence — physical, vital, mental and psychic — was inundated with my infinite Compassion-light. The rain that you were seeing was Grace, Compassion. The inner thrill that you felt was my wholehearted acceptance and immediate recognition of you that day. Your dream signifies my total acceptance of your spiritual life. I have hundreds of disciples. Some try to judge me; some absurdly attempt to fathom my spirituality, and some wait to see whether I can please them. On very rare occasions people do accept me immediately as you have done.

Remember your highest meditation.
Then with your determination
And eagerness,
Give life to that imagination.

About the author

Sri Chinmoy was born in the village of Shakpura in East Bengal, India (now Bangladesh) in 1931. He was the youngest of seven children in a devout family. In 1944, after the passing of both of his parents, he joined his brothers and sisters at the Sri Aurobindo Ashram, a spiritual community near Pondicherry in South India. He meditated for several hours a day, having many deep inner experiences. It was here that he first began writing poetry to convey his widening mystical vision. He also took an active part in Ashram life and was a champion athlete for many years.

Heeding an inner command, Sri Chinmoy moved to the United States in 1964 to be of service to spiritual aspirants in the Western world. During the 43 years that he lived in the West he opened more than 100 meditation Centres worldwide and served as spiritual guide to thousands of students. Sri Chinmoy's boundless creativity found expression not only in poetry and other forms of literature, but also in musical composition and performance, art and sport. In each sphere he sought to convey the diverse experiences that comprise the spiritual journey: the search for truth and beauty, the struggle to transcend limitations, and the supremely fulfilling communion of the human soul with the Divine.

As a self-described student of peace who combined Eastern spirituality and Western dynamism in a remarkable way, Sri Chinmoy garnered international renown. In 1970 at the request of U Thant, the third Secretary-General of the United Nations, he began the twice-weekly peace meditations for delegates and staff members at UN headquarters that continued until the end of his life. Sri Chinmoy enjoyed a special friendship with many international luminaries including President Mikhail Gorbachev, Mother Teresa, President Nelson Mandela and Archbishop Desmond Tutu.

On 11 October 2007, Sri Chinmoy passed behind the curtain of Eternity. His creative, peace-loving and humanitarian endeavours are carried on worldwide by his students, who practise meditation and strive to serve the world in accordance with his timeless teachings.

For more information about Sri Chinmoy kindly visit **www.srichinmoy.org**

*Learn to meditate
with the Sri Chinmoy Centre*

Sri Chinmoy Centres give meditation classes in over 350 cities all over the world. Sri Chinmoy asked his students to offer these classes to the general public free of charge, as he felt that the inner peace that meditation could bring was the birthright of each individual.

Find a meditation class near you on
www.srichinmoycentre.org

Recommended books by Sri Chinmoy

Seeking Perfect Health
Spiritual Secrets to Staying Healthy

This comprehensive book addresses the spiritual secrets of health by considering the connection between mind and body, health and karma, how to receive life energy from healthy diet and sleep, dealing with stress and depression, exercises for losing weight and overcoming insomnia, why a healthy body is important for spiritual practice and many other relevant topics.

(www.bluebeyondbooks.co.uk)

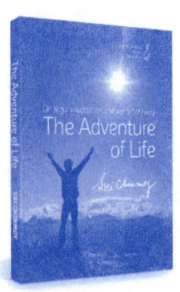

The Adventure of Life
On Yoga, Meditation, and the Art of Living

A modern-day spiritual manual that encourages the reader to embrace new ideas, adding a deeper, spiritual dimension to one's life.

In a clear and accessible way, Sri Chinmoy speaks about the spiritual art of living, society and religion as well as popular topics such as chakras, occult powers and the end of the world, and introduces us to a modern spiritual lifestyle with focus on health, diet, sport, family life and the workplace.

(**www.lifeadventure.net**)

Sport & Meditation
The Inner Dimension of Sport

This is a unique book, which challenges our preconceptions of our physical capacities and of the limitations of age. It includes specific exercises concerning meditation, concentration and mantra as aids to the focus needed in all forms of exercise and training. It is this new facet that enables us to achieve peak performance, to get more from exercise and to enjoy robust and lasting health and wellbeing.

World champions such as Carl Lewis, Tatyana Lebedeva, Tegla Loroupe, Bill Pearl, and Paul Tergat share their own inner secrets and spiritual perspectives on training and competition in anecdotes peppered throughout the book.

(**www.sportandmeditation.com**)

222 Meditation Techniques

These 222 guided exercises, the largest collection of meditation techniques in one book, are suitable for both beginners and advanced seekers who wish to explore the world of meditation. From breathing exercises, guided meditations and the use of mantras, to special exercises for runners, artists and musicians, ways to overcome depression, stress and bad habits, and even losing weight, this book offers a truly broad canvas of possibilities.

(**www.themeditationbook.net**)

Angels and Fairies

In this beautifully illustrated book Sri Chinmoy offers profound insight into the connection between angels and fairies and the role that these beings play in relation to us, with the confidence of someone who has attained free access to the inner realms.

(**www.bluebeyondbooks.co.uk**)

A Child's Heart and a Child's Dreams
Growing up with spiritual wisdom

This inspiring guide for both parents and children offers practical advice on a subject that concerns many conscious parents: fostering their child's spiritual life, watching him or her grow up with a love of God and a heart of self-giving, bringing up a balanced and kind person.

(**www.bluebeyondbooks.co.uk**)

Astrology, the Supernatural and the Beyond

In the course of his numerous public meditations and university lectures around the world, Sri Chinmoy was asked thousands of questions on occultism, astrology, flying saucers, extraterrestrial beings and similar subjects. This book presents some of the most interesting of these questions and Sri Chinmoy's answers.

(**www.bluebeyondbooks.co.uk**)

Heart-Wisdom-Drops
Inspiring Aphorisms for Every Day

This collection of 55 inspirational cards makes an excellent gift. Each card features an aphorism and meditative painting by Sri Chinmoy. For those seeking hope, peace of mind and life-wisdom these cards offer inspiration, and are a guide to a happy, harmonious and spiritually-grounded daily life.

(**www.wisdom-cards.com**)

For more books kindly visit
www.bluebeyondbooks.co.uk